I0815554

THE 1990s
THROUGH THE DECADES
BY CHRISTINA LEAF
eureka!

Eureka! books turn real stories into unforgettable experiences. This nonfiction imprint sparks curiosity, encourages critical thinking, and engages middle-grade readers. *Eureka!* books empower young minds to explore the stories of the real world, one fascinating fact at a time. Unravel the power of knowledge and lifelong learning with *Eureka!*

This edition first published in 2026 by Bellwether Media, Inc.

Library of Congress Cataloging-in-Publication Data

LC record for The 1990s available at: https://lccn.loc.gov/2025021827

Editor: Rebecca Sabelko Designer: Andrea Schneider

Printed in the United States of America, North Mankato, MN.

TABLE OF CONTENTS

WELCOME TO THE 1990s!

It is a sunny afternoon in 1997. A kid slips headphones over his ears as he walks home from the bus stop. The latest Backstreet Boys album plays on his portable CD player. He stops by the mailbox to pick up the mail. His new issue of *Sports Illustrated for Kids* has arrived! Brett Favre is on the cover. In the kitchen, he grabs a pack of Gushers for a snack. Then, he heads to the family room to play some *Super Mario 64* on his Nintendo 64. At 5 o'clock, he turns on a rerun of his favorite TV show, *Are You Afraid of the Dark?*

The phone rings while his family is eating dinner. Some of the neighbor kids are going to play games after dark. He throws on an oversized sweatshirt, laces up his Nikes, and joins them for ghost in the graveyard and flashlight tag. Before bed, he reads a couple of chapters in the latest Goosebumps book. He is a true '90s kid!

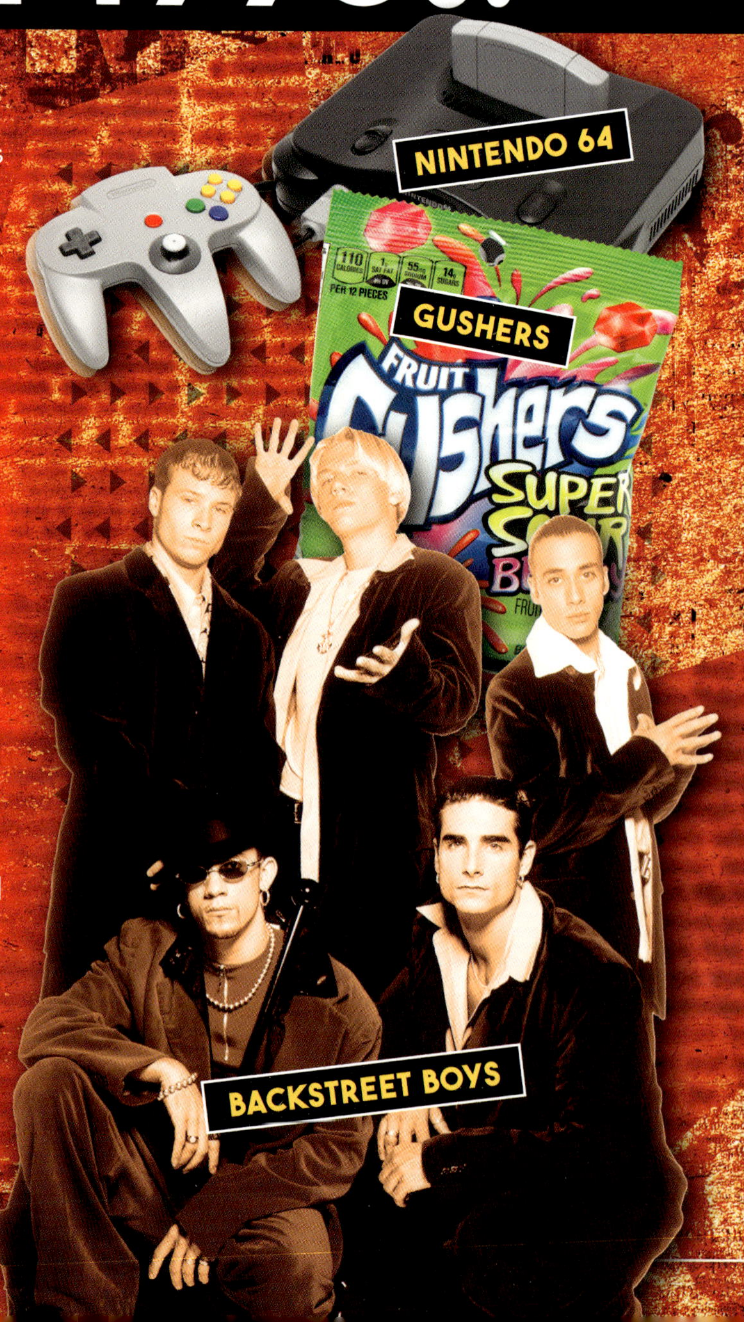

Are You Afraid
of the Dark? Cast

WHAT HAPPENED IN THE 1990s?

The 1990s are often thought of as a time of peace and prosperity. One of the biggest influences on the decade was the end of the **Cold War** due to the fall of the **Soviet Union** in 1991. The previous decades had been marked with the threat of possible **nuclear war** between the United States and the Soviet Union. With the collapse of the Soviet Union, the U.S. became the most powerful country in the world. It often used its role to try to act as a peacemaker in conflicts.

The U.S. experienced an economic boom after the Cold War ended. Many markets found huge success, particularly the relatively new computer and technology market. It created new jobs and frequent demand for upgraded products as technology improved. This brought new wealth, particularly among a small number of people.

This new wealth created a **skepticism** of businesses, especially in younger people. They warned against consumerism and **selling out**. They believed that working with big corporations and changing one's beliefs and art to make money made someone shallow and fake.

HOW MUCH?

1 GALLON GAS

$1.15 (1990)
$1.17 (1999)

THE NEW YORK TIMES

(daily national edition in New York)

$0.40 (1990) | $0.60 (1999)

MOVIE TICKET

$4.22 (1990)
$5.06 (1999)

HALF GALLON ICE CREAM

$2.72 (1990)
$3.40 (1999)

LOAF OF BREAD

$0.69 (1990)
$0.90 (1999)

1 GALLON MILK

$2.78 (1990)
$2.88 (1999)

2-LITER BOTTLE OF COKE

$0.89 (1991)
$1.03 (1999)

HISTORY

LOS ANGELES RIOTS

UNITED STATES HISTORY

Despite the popular idea that the 1990s was a peaceful decade, there was a lot of turmoil in the U.S. Early in the decade, the U.S. fought against Iraq in the Persian Gulf War. Thanks to CNN, people across the globe could get live, 24/7 television coverage of the war. The conflict was not the only trouble the U.S. faced in the first half of the '90s. The country continued to struggle with the **AIDS** crisis that began in the 1980s. A **recession** also followed the Persian Gulf War.

The country saw violence on its own land. **Riots** shook Los Angeles in 1992. In 1993, **terrorists** bombed the World Trade Center in New York. Violence reached the nation's schools as two students shot classmates and teachers at Columbine High School in Colorado in 1999.

WORLD TRADE CENTER AFTER 1993 BOMBING

MEMORIAL SITE FOR COLUMBINE SHOOTING VICTIMS

PERSIAN GULF WAR

In August 1990, Iraqi leader Saddam Hussein invaded Kuwait and seemed ready to move into Saudi Arabia. The U.S. and other countries bombed Iraq, and just over one month later, they sent in troops. Troop fighting lasted fewer than five days, but trouble in the region continued long after the war ended in 1991.

Saddam Hussein

THE OKLAHOMA CITY BOMBING

On April 19, 1995, a bomb exploded in a van outside of the Alfred P. Murrah Federal Building in Oklahoma City. The attack killed 168 people and became the deadliest terrorist attack on U.S. soil at the time. The bomber was a Gulf War veteran who was angry at the government. He was caught shortly after the bombing.

THE O.J. SIMPSON TRIAL

In 1995, former National Football League (NFL) star O.J. Simpson was on trial, accused of murdering his ex-wife and a waiter. Around 150 million television viewers watched as lawyers asked him to try on gloves likely worn by the killer. But the gloves did not seem to fit. Simpson was **acquitted**, though many remained unconvinced.

O.J. Simpson

UNITED STATES POLITICS

The year 1990 began with George H.W. Bush as U.S. president. During this time, he signed a deal for a trade agreement between the U.S., Canada, and Mexico called the North American Free Trade Agreement. He also appointed Justice Clarence Thomas to the U.S. Supreme Court. However, a recession and Bush's decision to raise taxes made him lose popularity. In the 1992 election, Democrat Bill Clinton was elected as the 42nd U.S. president.

President George H.W. Bush

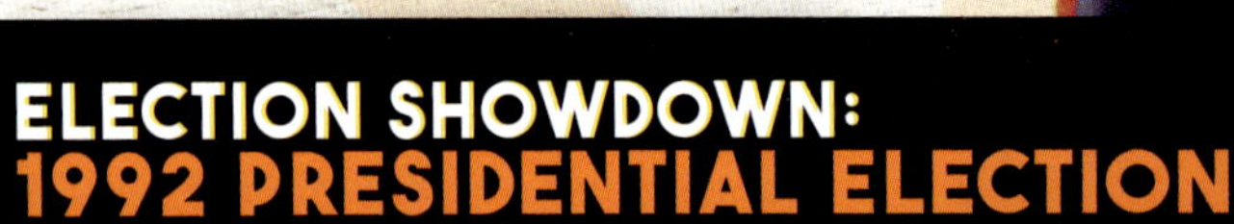

CLINTON (DEMOCRATIC)

BUSH (REPUBLICAN)

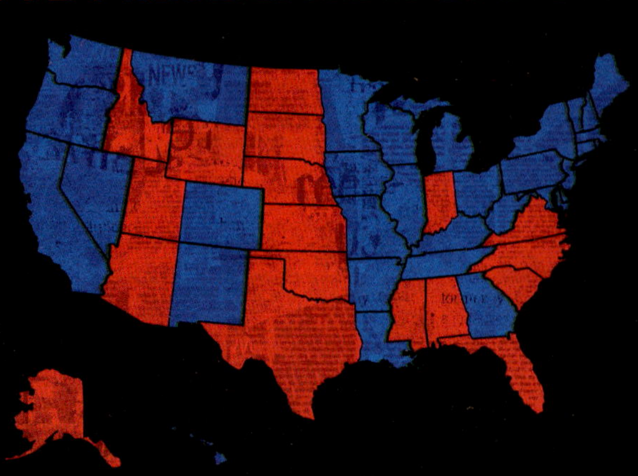

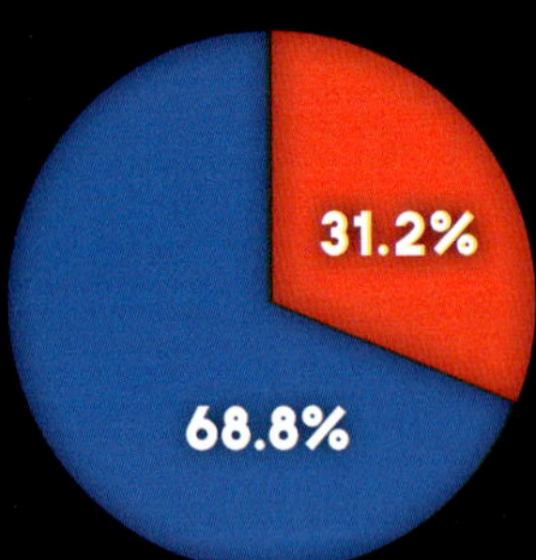

ELECTORAL VOTES

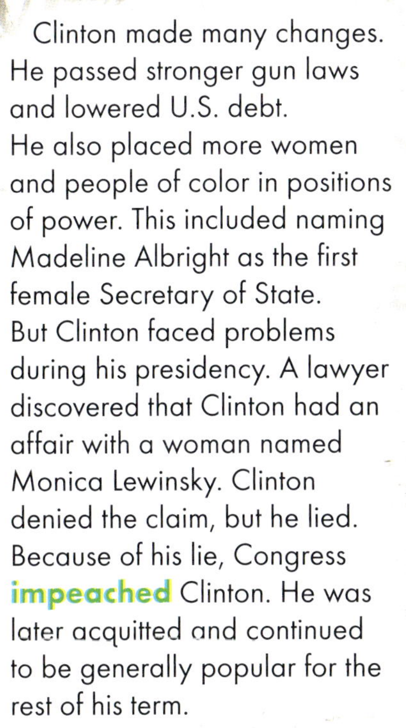

Clinton made many changes. He passed stronger gun laws and lowered U.S. debt. He also placed more women and people of color in positions of power. This included naming Madeline Albright as the first female Secretary of State. But Clinton faced problems during his presidency. A lawyer discovered that Clinton had an affair with a woman named Monica Lewinsky. Clinton denied the claim, but he lied. Because of his lie, Congress **impeached** Clinton. He was later acquitted and continued to be generally popular for the rest of his term.

JUSTICE CLARENCE THOMAS

SECRETARY OF STATE MADELINE ALBRIGHT

MONICA LEWINSKY

Ross Perot

THIRD-PARTY CANDIDATE

In the 1992 presidential election, Ross Perot ran as a third-party candidate. Though he did not win any states, he managed to take 19 percent of the popular vote. This was the most successful third-party run since 1912!

SPOTLIGHT ON:

RODNEY KING AND THE LOS ANGELES RIOTS

Early in the morning of March 3, 1991, four white Los Angeles police officers stopped driver Rodney King. When King, who was Black, was slow to respond to the officers' demands, the officers began to kick King, beat him with batons, and tase him. A witness caught the beating on tape, and it was soon on the news. The officers went to trial for excessive use of force. On April 29, 1992, a nearly all-white **jury** with no Black jurors acquitted the officers on all counts except one.

People were furious. Protesters gathered in South Central Los Angeles, and violence soon broke out. People began **looting** businesses and setting fire to buildings. The Los Angeles mayor set a curfew on the first night, but riots continued for five days. On May 1, President Bush sent in military troops, and on May 3, things began to calm down. The riots brought more than 50 deaths, thousands of injuries, and nearly $1 billion worth of damage. But they also brought national attention to the issue of **racism** against Black Americans.

MAKING HEADLINES

"All 4 in King Beating Acquitted – Violence Follows Verdicts; Guard Called Out"

–*LA Times*, April 30, 1992

"LOOTING AND FIRES RAVAGE L.A. – 25 DEAD, 572 INJURED; 1,000 BLAZES REPORTED"

–*LA TIMES*, MAY 1, 1992

"Rodney King Asks, 'Can We All Get Along?'"

–*The New York Times*, May 1, 1992

building on fire during the Los Angeles riots

WORLD HISTORY

The 1990s was a decade of major changes across the globe. The breakups of the Soviet Union and Yugoslavia resulted in several countries forming or regaining independence. Peace came to the U.S. and western Europe with the end of the Cold War. The creation of the European Union furthered that peace in Europe. The end of **apartheid** changed South Africa. Communication continued to improve throughout the world, connecting countries more easily and bringing new trade agreements. The global economy also brought unexpected consequences, such as a financial crisis in Asia causing worldwide effects.

Suffering and violence shook parts of the world. Rwanda and Bosnia faced horrific **genocides**. Hurricane Mitch devastated parts of Central America. The Persian Gulf War brought thousands of Iraqi deaths. While many Western countries managed the AIDS crisis with new treatments, African countries did not have access to the same treatments, and the disease swept the continent.

PROTESTING TO END APARTHEID

DEVASTATION LEFT BY HURRICANE MITCH

SOLDIERS SERVING DURING THE PERSIAN GULF WAR

APARTHEID AND NELSON MANDELA

South Africa functioned under apartheid for many years. This policy separated South Africans by race. Most South Africans disagreed with apartheid, and many protested it. One anti-apartheid leader, Nelson Mandela, was jailed for his actions for nearly 30 years. Mandela was released in 1990. He worked with the all-white government to end apartheid. In 1991, the government removed most laws related to apartheid. Mandela was elected the first Black president of South Africa in 1994.

Nelson Mandela

Diana, Princess of Wales

THE PEOPLE'S PRINCESS

On August 31, 1997, Diana, Princess of Wales died due to injuries from a car crash. Diana was hugely popular, even after her divorce from Prince Charles. She was known for her charity work, particularly with AIDS patients at a time when much was unknown about the disease. As many as 2.5 billion people watched her funeral on television.

RWANDAN GENOCIDE

Relations between the two main ethnic groups in Rwanda, the Hutus and the Tutsis, were bad for decades. In 1994, a plane carrying Juvénal Habyarimana, the Rwandan president and a Hutu, was shot down. The Hutus blamed the Tutsis and killed hundreds of thousands of Tutsis in just 100 days. A Tutsi group eventually took control and stopped the killing, but the country has still not fully healed.

SPOTLIGHT ON:

THE COLLAPSE OF THE SOVIET UNION

The Soviet Union was a global superpower through much of the 20th century. It was made up of 15 **republics** under the control of a **Communist** government based in Moscow. But in the 1980s, the Soviet Union was losing power. Soviet leader Mikhail Gorbachev made new democratic policies to strengthen the economy and keep the country together. These new laws gave republics more freedom. In 1989, many republics began demanding independence. Some Communists did not like what was happening in the country. They tried to overthrow Gorbachev. They were unsuccessful, thanks in part to Russian leader Boris Yeltsin. But Gorbachev had lost control of the country. On December 25, 1991, Gorbachev resigned as president of the Soviet Union. On December 31, the Soviet Union ceased to exist.

The collapse had worldwide effects. The Cold War was definitively over, which brought better relations between the U.S. and Russia for a time. Former Soviet republics gained independence. But many struggled with economic independence, and revolts happened in these countries, including Russia. Tensions also remained between some Soviet states. Some continue today.

MAKING HEADLINES

"End of the Soviet Union; The Soviet State, Born of a Dream, Dies"

—*The New York Times*, December 26, 1991

"GORBACHEV, LAST SOVIET LEADER, RESIGNS"

—*THE NEW YORK TIMES*, DECEMBER 26, 1991

WHO'S WHO?

MIKHAIL GORBACHEV

ROLE:

President of the Soviet Union (1990 to 1991)

KNOWN FOR:

Gorbachev was the last leader of the Soviet Union who lifted the Iron Curtain, allowed for more rights within the Soviet Union, and worked with President Ronald Reagan to end the Cold War.

BORIS YELTSIN

ROLE:

President of Russia (1991 to 1999)

KNOWN FOR:

Yeltsin was the first elected head of state in Russia who became the leader of Russia after the fall of the Soviet Union. He condemned the overthrow of Gorbachev and called for a strike while standing on a tank.

SOCIAL CHANGES

Civil rights in the U.S. faced a setback when President Bush **vetoed** the Civil Rights Act of 1990. It would have helped people who had been **discriminated** against in their jobs. The 1992 riots in Los Angeles also showed the need for more change. But there were advancements that created positive change for people of color. President Clinton created the most **diverse** cabinet to date when he took office. People of color won major awards, governed cities and states, and led major businesses. Woman gained roles in positions of power, too. But attitudes began to doubt the women's rights movement. People worried that families were falling apart because more women were working.

People with disabilities also experienced positive changes. In 1990, President Bush signed the Americans with Disabilities Act (ADA). This law says people and businesses cannot discriminate against people who have disabilities. Its aim is to make it easier for people with disabilities to get jobs, access buildings, and ride public transportation.

President Bill Clinton

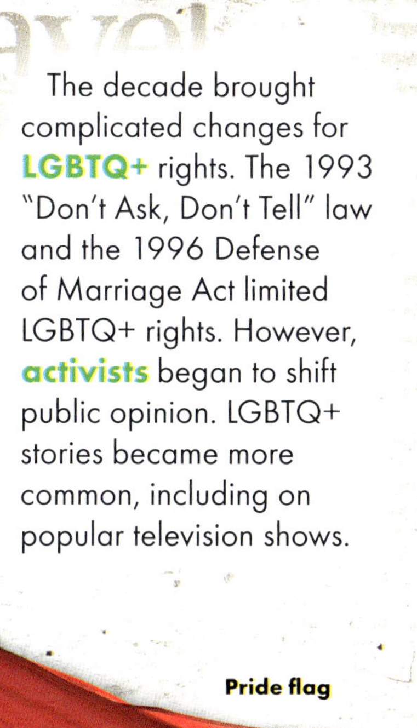

The decade brought complicated changes for **LGBTQ+** rights. The 1993 "Don't Ask, Don't Tell" law and the 1996 Defense of Marriage Act limited LGBTQ+ rights. However, **activists** began to shift public opinion. LGBTQ+ stories became more common, including on popular television shows.

PRESIDENT BUSH SIGNING THE ADA

Pride flag

LGBTQ+ ACTIVISTS

WILL & GRACE, AN LGBTQ+ TV SHOW

FEELING PROUD

In June 1999, President Clinton declared the first Gay and Lesbian Pride Month.

SCIENCE AND TECHNOLOGY

TECHNOLOGY

The 1990s saw rapid advancements in technology. Computers changed dramatically. New technology made them smaller and cheaper. This made them more accessible to the average person. Between 1990 and 1997, computer ownership in the U.S. more than doubled. Laptops grew more popular, and personal digital assistants that could fit in the palm of a hand were introduced.

The World Wide Web became publicly available in 1993. It would eventually affect nearly every aspect of daily life. The Web made it easy for personal computer users to get online. Soon, users could find websites to help with many tasks, including communicating with people through email and getting their daily news. By the end of the decade, people could find information on nearly any topic with Google. Amazon would soon become a major online retailer.

WORLD WIDE WEB

WHAT IS IT?:
A network of web pages on the internet accessed through addresses and often connected by hyperlinks

INVENTOR:
Tim Berners-Lee

YEAR INVENTED:
1989

EFFECT ON DAILY LIFE:
Changed the way people communicate, shop, find information, get news, and much, much more

The growing dependence on computers did pose some problems. One major concern was the Y2K bug. Computers were programmed using 2-digit numbers to represent a year, such as 90 instead of 1990. People worried that computers would recognize the year 2000 as 1900. This could cause problems in banks, power plants, and other industries. However, very few problems arose from the new year.

ON THE PHONE

People in the 1990s connected to the internet through their phone lines. They could not talk on the phone and use the internet at the same time.

Y2K New Year's Eve Celebration

SCIENTIFIC DISCOVERIES

Big discoveries were made in the scientific world in the 1990s. One of the most important was the Human Genome Project. This effort worked to figure out the chemistry of human **DNA**. Scientists hoped this knowledge would help make better medicines and tell if people were at risk for harmful diseases. The project began in 1990. By the end of the decade, scientists completed a sequence of one **chromosome**. They would complete the project in 2003.

Another major development involved a sheep named Dolly. In 1997, British scientist Dr. Ian Wilmut announced that he created an exact clone of an adult sheep from a single cell. The clone was named Dolly. Some people were excited about the possibilities of cloning other animals to produce more food. Cloning could also help create medicines or new organs or tissues for people. But some people worried about the potential of cloning humans in the future.

Other discoveries were much farther from home. On April 24, 1990, the Hubble Space Telescope was launched. It allowed us to peer farther into space than ever before, giving us pictures of galaxies, stars, and planetary systems. It also gave proof that supermassive black holes exist!

ILLUSTRATION OF DNA INSIDE A CHROMOSOME

DR. IAN WILMUT WITH DOLLY THE SHEEP

HUBBLE SPACE TELESCOPE

T-RIFFIC!

On August 12, 1990, scientist Susan Hendrickson discovered one of the largest and most complete Tyrannosaurus rex fossils ever found. Today, the skeleton stands tall in Chicago's Field Museum. It is named Sue after its discoverer!

Tyrannosaurus rex fossil, Sue, in Chicago's Field Museum

DAILY LIFE

LIFE IN THE '90s

The wealth of the 1990s saw the middle class increase, particularly for Black families. However, many households still relied on both parents working. The number of families with one parent, which had been growing in previous years, went down slightly. **Multigenerational** housing, which included grandparents, started to become more common.

Suburban areas grew as more families moved out of rural and urban areas. Newer suburbs had large houses that were often mass-produced. For getting around, Sport Utility Vehicles (SUVs) became a popular car choice, especially for families. Wal-Mart rapidly grew in popularity for its low prices and focus on rural and suburban areas. Malls were also popular places to shop.

Technology became more accessible. Most people still had landline phones, but cell phones became more common. Kids began to access the internet. Adults began to worry about online safety and privacy.

SPORT UTILITY VEHICLE

WAL-MART

USING A CELL PHONE

1990s SLANG

said after a statement to change what you said and turn it into an insult

Talk to the hand!

I'm not going to listen anymore; usually said with an outstretched hand in a "stop" gesture

No duh

of course, usually implying this was obvious

HARSH

unnecessarily mean or bad

BOOYAH

an exclamation to celebrate joy or success

As if

a reaction to say something is unlikely to be true

made popular by the 1995 movie, *Clueless*

'Sup

What's up? How are you?

FLY

really cool

FASHION TRENDS

Fashion in the 1990s moved away from the **maximalist** fashion of the 1980s. On the runways and red carpets, many fashion designers opted for sleek, simple designs. Supermodels popularized slip dresses with spaghetti straps. Black and other muted colors were common, especially in mall stores such as Gap.

One major change in the 1990s was the trend toward casual clothing in business. New computer companies with younger workers opted for less formal clothing. Soon, casual Fridays became popular at older companies, too.

GAP

slip dress with spaghetti straps

Many trends were connected to popular music of the decade. Hip-hop culture was one of the largest drivers of fashion trends. Baggy jeans and T-shirts were often paired with Timberland boots, bucket hats, and puffy jackets. Hip-hop artists also helped make Starter jackets wildly popular. The jackets were usually branded with the logos of different professional sports teams. Grunge fans tended toward plaid flannel shirts, worn-out jeans, and chunky Doc Martens.

Pop culture brought popular hairstyles, too. *Friends* had women heading to the salon to ask for the "Rachel." Micro braids were common thanks to singer and *Moesha* actor Brandy. Many men sported hair with bleached ends, known as frosted tips. Justin Timberlake was one celebrity with this style during the decade.

Doc Martens

GRUNGE FASHION

BUCKET HAT

THE "RACHEL"

PRODUCTS AND TOYS

Toys in the 1990s become more and more electronic. Beyond video games, toys like digital pets, diaries, and games all required batteries. But there were still many favorite unplugged toys. Kids had a lot of variety in this **transitional** decade!

Pokémon trading cards

Sony PlayStation

POKÉMON

In 1996, the first Pokémon video games were released in Japan. The trading card game quickly became popular, too. Kids could collect and trade cards of different creatures. Then, they used the cards to battle other players.

VIDEO GAME CONSOLES

Video game consoles kept improving in the 1990s. Nintendo first released the Super Nintendo in 1990 and the Nintendo 64 in 1996. The handheld Game Boy Color came out in 1998. Sega kept up with the Saturn in 1994 and the Dreamcast in 1998. Sony released the PlayStation in 1994.

FURBY

A fluffy robotic toy called Furby was first introduced in 1998. This toy could speak and move its eyes, ears, and mouth. It reacted to being petted.

BEANIE BABIES

Beanie Babies debuted in 1993. These plush toys were filled with plastic pellets and shaped like different animals. Each one had a tag with its name. Later, each tag included a poem and birthdate.

POGS

Kids collected cardboard circles called pogs in the 1990s. To play pogs, each player added facedown pogs to a stack. Then, they took turns throwing thick, heavy slammers onto the stack. Any pogs that got turned over by a player were theirs to keep!

TAMAGOTCHI

Tamagotchis were digital pets on keychains. They first came out in Japan in 1996. Owners needed to care for their pets, or they would die.

GAK

Gak was a rubbery, slime-like toy made by Mattel and Nickelodeon. Kids could stretch it, bounce it, blow bubbles in it, and make fart sounds with it. First introduced in 1992, Gak soon came in a number of variations, including glow-in-the-dark Gak and color-changing Gak.

ARTS AND ENTERTAINMENT

PUBLICATIONS

In the 1990s, books faced fierce competition as children's entertainment, with television and the growing popularity of computers and video games. Still, many series were popular among young readers. Kids tore through R. L. Stine's Goosebumps and Fear Street books. Animorphs and the Babysitter's Club were also hits. Scholastic Book Fairs and book orders continued to be popular ways for kids to find and buy books.

The decade saw the growth of big chain bookstores, such as Barnes & Noble and Borders. Barnes & Noble expanded across the country, taking over smaller chains as it grew. It also began to include Starbucks coffee shops, which led people to linger in the stores. Amazon began as an online bookstore in the 1990s, making the internet a new avenue for book buying.

READING REC

TITLE:
HOLES

AUTHOR:
Louis Sachar

YEAR PUBLISHED:
1998

SUMMARY:
After being wrongly accused of theft, teen Stanley Yelnats is sent to the correctional Camp Green Lake in the Texas desert.

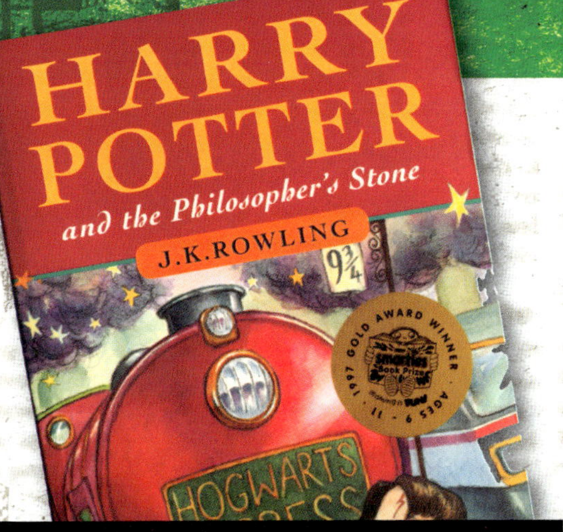

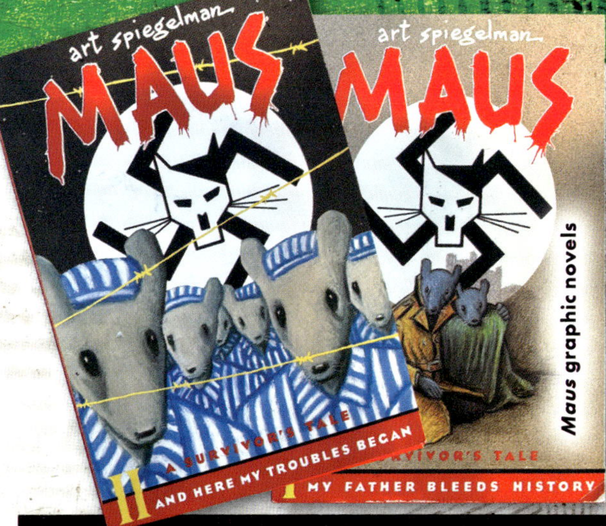

Maus graphic novels

HARRY POTTER

Harry Potter and the Philosopher's Stone was first published in the United Kingdom in 1997. By its publication in the U.S. in 1998, it had become a sensation. The Harry Potter series brought a new popularity to reading that extended beyond the series. The series also brought new respect for children's books. This led to the creation of a children's bestseller list in *The New York Times*.

GRAPHIC NOVELS

Graphic novels and comics continued to become more respected in the 1990s. *Maus* became the first graphic novel to win a Pulitzer Prize in 1992. The decade also saw most of The decade also saw the introduction of Deadpool to comic books.

MAGAZINES

A wealth of magazines aimed at kids and teens started in the 1990s. Some were general, like *American Girl* and *Girl's Life*. Others, such as *Disney Adventures* and *Nickelodeon* magazine, were based on popular television channels. Popular adult magazines made versions for younger readers, such as *CosmoGirl* and *Teen People*.

Oprah Winfrey

OPRAH'S BOOK CLUB

One of the biggest influences on book sales in the 1990s was TV host Oprah Winfrey. In 1996, she began announcing picks for her book club that she would later discuss on her show. Sales skyrocketed for book club picks. Winfrey's diverse picks also helped **genres** like literary fiction regain popularity.

MOVIES

The 1990s brought a wide range of movie experiences. Multi-screened theaters called megaplexes became common. People flocked to megaplexes to see blockbuster movies with top-of-the-line visual effects. Independent films also saw a bump in popularity. This was partly due to anti-corporate attitudes, especially in young people. More screens also allowed more independent movies to be distributed. The internet allowed independent movies to market to more people.

At home, people watched VHS tapes. Video stores such as Blockbuster were common and allowed people to rent tapes, usually for one or two days. By the end of the decade, DVDs had debuted in the U.S. Soon after, Netflix was created. This service allowed people to rent DVDs that were delivered through the mail.

AT THE BOX OFFICE

TOP-GROSSING FILMS OF THE 1990s

- ***Titanic*** **(1997)**
- ***Jurassic Park*** **(1993)**
- ***Star Wars: Episode I - The Phantom Menace*** **(1999)**
- ***The Lion King*** **(1994)**
- ***Independence Day*** **(1996)**
- ***Forrest Gump*** **(1994)**
- ***The Sixth Sense*** **(1999)**
- ***The Lost World: Jurassic Park*** **(1997)**
- ***Men in Black*** **(1997)**
- ***Armageddon*** **(1998)**

Jurassic Park

The Lion King

DISNEY RENAISSANCE

Disney animated movies saw a huge jump in popularity in the 1990s. Movies such as *Aladdin, The Lion King*, and *Mulan* were favorites with viewers and critics alike. *Beauty and the Beast* was the first animated movie to be nominated for the Academy Award for Best Picture!

CGI ANIMATED MOVIES

Computer-generated imagery (CGI) animation reached new heights in the 1990s. Animators could easily use computers to make 3D scenes. Pixar was the first company to release a full-length movie made entirely with this technology. *Toy Story*, released in 1995, was a huge hit! This inspired other companies, such as DreamWorks, to release similar movies.

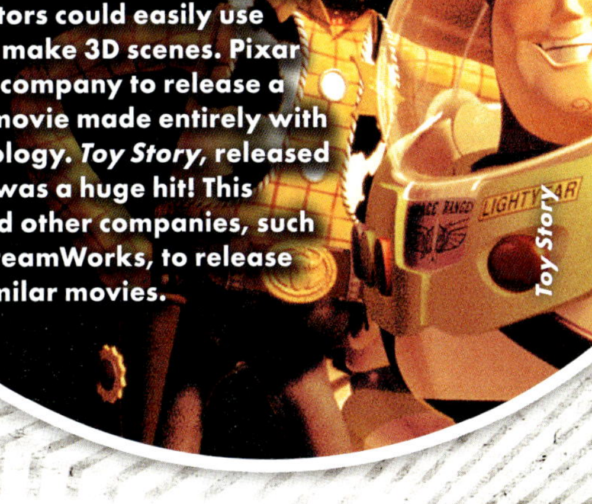

Toy Story

TITANIC

Costing more than $200 million, *Titanic* was the most expensive movie ever made at the time. But it made all of that back and more. It was the top-grossing movie of all time for more than 10 years. It also tied records for the most nominations and wins for the Academy Awards.

VISUAL EFFECTS

Computer technology allowed movies to look more realistic than ever. *Jurassic Park* was one of the first. It combined real models with CGI animation to bring dinosaurs to life. *Titanic* used computer technology to recreate the sinking of the *Titanic*. Jar-Jar Binks of *Star Wars: Episode I - The Phantom Menace*, became the first major character fully created by motion capture and CGI.

Jar-Jar Binks

THE PHANTOM MENACE

One of the most awaited movies of the 1990s was *Star Wars: Episode I - The Phantom Menace*. People could not wait to see the first new Star Wars movie in more than 15 years. Some people bought tickets to other movies just to see the Star Wars trailer!

TELEVISION

Television changed quickly in the 1990s due to cable television's continued growth. People had access to channels with more specific programming. Some channels, like HBO, offered edgier content that could not air on network television. Networks competed by creating blocks of popular shows such as NBC's "Must See TV." These blocks were designed to get viewers to tune in before and after popular shows.

By the end of the decade, the introduction of TiVo began an even bigger shift in television. This device allowed people to record programs digitally. It was a forerunner to the eventual switch to streaming.

The Sopranos, HBO

The Real World, Season 1

THE REAL WORLD

In 1992, *The Real World* premiered on MTV. It followed a group of strangers who lived in an apartment together. *The Real World* was one of the first reality shows. It also broke ground by discussing subjects like race, sexuality, and women's rights.

Seinfeld

SITCOMS

Several influential and popular sitcoms aired in the 1990s. *The Simpsons* brought new respect to animation for adults and inspired many new shows in the medium. *Seinfeld* centered on a group of friends instead of a family. Its focus on everyday problems made it one of the most popular shows of the decade. *Friends* emphasized the importance of friendship while also starting fashion and other cultural trends.

The Ren & Stimpy Show

NICKELODEON

Nickelodeon's kid-focused approach made it extremely popular. In 1991, it introduced *Doug*, *Rugrats*, and *The Ren & Stimpy Show*. These original cartoons were huge hits! The network soon added more animated shows, later known as Nicktoons. Nickelodeon also had game shows and shows that highlighted relatable kids and teens.

The Fresh Prince of Bel-Air

TEEN SHOWS

Teen dramas had a golden age in the 1990s, starting with the popular *Beverly Hills 90210*. Later shows focused more on middle-class, relatable teens, such as *Party of Five* and *Dawson's Creek*. By the end of the decade, shows like *Buffy the Vampire Slayer* brought in supernatural elements.

BLACK COMEDIES

The success of *The Cosby Show* in the 1980s spurred on a new wave of sitcoms featuring Black stories in the 1990s. *The Fresh Prince of Bel-Air*, *Moesha*, *Living Single*, and *Sister, Sister* were some of the popular shows created. But by the end of the decade, viewership began to drop.

MUSIC

All kinds of music gained mainstream popularity in the decade. Hip-hop, which had continued to grow through the 1980s, became dominant. R&B artists including Whitney Houston, Boyz II Men, and Mariah Carey also enjoyed massive popularity. Grunge rock, characterized by angry lyrics and **distorted** guitars, evolved from punk and metal influences. Teen pop saw a comeback, while country music went through changes.

The decade ushered in the transition from cassette tapes to compact discs (CDs). Sales for CDs outpaced cassettes in the early 1990s. People could take their CDs on the go in the car or with portable Discman players.

Whitney Houston

1990s PLAYLIST

- ***Friends in Low Places***
  Garth Brooks (1990)
- ***Smells Like Teen Spirit***
  Nirvana (1991)
- ***I Will Always Love You***
  Whitney Houston (1992)
- ***Macarena***
  Los del Rio (1993)
- ***Always Be My Baby***
  Mariah Carey (1995)
- ***Wonderwall***
  Oasis (1995)
- ***Ironic***
  Alanis Morissette (1996)
- ***Wannabe***
  Spice Girls (1996)
- ***Gettin' Jiggy Wit It***
  Will Smith (1997)
- ***My Heart Will Go On***
  Celine Dion (1997)

Discman

Britney Spears

GRUNGE ROCK

Grunge rock started in the late 1980s in Seattle and reached peak popularity in the mid-1990s. Nirvana and Pearl Jam were two of the biggest grunge bands. The success of Nirvana's 1991 album, *Nevermind*, shook up mainstream culture and connected young people across the world. The style would lead to new types of alternative rock.

Kurt Cobain of Nirvana

TEEN POP

In 1996, the British girl group the Spice Girls took the world by storm. Their popularity launched a new era of teen pop. Catchy hits from boy bands such as *NSYNC and the Backstreet Boys climbed the charts. Female vocalists including Britney Spears and Christina Aguilera also found success.

Shania Twain

COUNTRY

Country music began to see more mainstream success. Garth Brooks was one of the top-selling artists of the 1990s. His music blended country with rock influences. Artists such as Shania Twain brought pop elements to the music. Line dance songs like Billy Ray Cyrus's "Achy Breaky Heart" also defined the genre.

HIP-HOP

Hip-hop became the biggest-selling music genre by the mid-1990s. Artists such as Notorious B.I.G., 2Pac, and Jay-Z began to hit #1 on the *Billboard* charts. Later in the decade, artists such as Lauryn Hill and Eminem expanded and popularized the genre even further.

2Pac

MACARENA

In the mid-1990s, a dance craze swept the world. Spanish music duo Los del Rio released the song "Macarena" in 1993. A remix was released in 1995 that included some English lyrics along with the original Spanish. The song's music video highlighted an easy-to-learn dance. This new version climbed the U.S. charts and kept everyone dancing!

U.S. SPORTS

Sports were big business in the U.S. in the 1990s. More games and events were televised than ever before. Cost for attending games and events grew. Athletes and team owners were earning more than ever. **Endorsements** also increased player wealth.

Football continued to be the most popular sport in the U.S. The NFL expanded with two new teams in 1995. Basketball was also popular. Michael Jordan and the Chicago Bulls' dominance over the league helped the National Basketball Association (NBA) gain many fans. The star-studded Dream Team of the 1992 U.S. men's Olympic basketball team also boosted popularity worldwide. In 1997, the Women's National Basketball Association (WNBA) had its first game.

MVP

NAME:
MICHAEL JORDAN

SPORT:
Basketball

YEARS PLAYED:
1984 to 1998; 2001 to 2003

TEAMS:
Chicago Bulls and Washington Wizards

KNOWN FOR:
One of the greatest basketball players of all time, he led the Chicago Bulls to three back-to-back championships two times for six championships within eight years.

Sammy Sosa and Mark McGwire

STRIKES AND HOME RUNS

Major League Baseball (MLB) players went on strike in 1994. Players felt they were not getting paid fairly for the money they brought in. That year was only the second time the World Series was not held. Play resumed in 1995, but popularity was slow to return. Mark McGwire and Sammy Sosa battling for the home run record brought fans back in 1998.

BMX biking

THE X GAMES

The decade saw extreme sports such as BMX biking and skateboarding gain many fans. ESPN created the Extreme Games in 1995. Later known as the X Games, the games featured nine sports categories and 27 events. They were so popular, ESPN decided to host them every year.

TIGER WOODS

The professional golf world was turned upside down when a young golfer named Tiger Woods hit the links in 1996. In 1997, he became the first Black player to win the Masters Tournament. Woods encouraged many young people to take up the sport that had previously been more popular with older people. He also brought new athleticism to the game.

SERENA WILLIAMS

Serena Williams was only the second Black woman to win a Grand Slam singles title when she won the 1999 U.S. Open at age 17. Williams and her sister, Venus, had been playing professionally for years, but Venus had been marked as the better player. With her win, Serena showed the world that she would dominate tennis for years to come!

GLOBAL SPORTS

The 1990s brought big changes to international sports. The Summer and Winter Olympics were held in the same year for the last time in 1992. Barcelona, Spain, hosted the Summer Games and Albertville, France, hosted the Winter Games.

The FIFA World Cup continued to be popular. The U.S. hosted the competition in 1994. It saw the highest attendance of any World Cup! The 1990s also saw the start of the Women's World Cup in 1991. In 1999, the U.S. hosted the Women's World Cup. The tournament was larger and more publicized than ever, and the U.S. team's win saw a new era of women's soccer begin.

ITALIA 90 WORLD CUP

The 1990 FIFA World Cup in Italy had upsets and surprises, with West Germany winning the tournament. But perhaps the tournament's biggest impact came from England. The English team was knocked out on penalties in the semifinals. But the performance brought enthusiasm for soccer back to England. Just two years later, the Premier League was created. It is now the most-watched league in the world!

SCANDAL ON ICE

Figure skaters Nancy Kerrigan and Tonya Harding were fierce rivals in the 1990s. Weeks before the 1994 Olympics, Kerrigan was clubbed in the knee. Police soon found out that Harding's husband had hired the attacker. They guessed that Harding may have been involved, too. Despite the injury, Kerrigan went on to take the silver medal while Harding took eighth.

Nancy Kerrigan

Kerri Strug

Brandi Chastain

1999 WOMEN'S WORLD CUP

The final of the 1999 Women's World Cup between China and the U.S. was tight. The game came to a penalty shootout. U.S. goalie Briana Scurry saved the third shot from China, leaving Brandi Chastain to drive home the final U.S. goal for the win. They were the first team to win the Women's World Cup in their home country!

VAULTING TO VICTORY

In Atlanta in 1996, the U.S. Gymnastics team was close to winning the first ever all-around Olympic gold medal for the country. But their lead was slipping. They needed a strong vault from Kerri Strug. On her first vault, Strug hurt her ankle. Still, she set up for her second vault. She flipped, twisted, and stuck the landing, winning gold for the U.S.

TIMELINE

APRIL 24, 1990
The Hubble Space Telescope is launched

JULY 26, 1990
President Bush signs the Americans with Disabilities Act

AUGUST 12, 1990
Susan Hendrickson discovers one of the largest and most complete Tyrannosaurus rex fossils in South Dakota

JUNE 17, 1991
The South African government repeals apartheid

NOVEMBER 1991
The first FIFA Women's World Cup is held

DECEMBER 25, 1991
Mikhail Gorbachev steps down as leader of the Soviet Union and the country ceases to exist less than a week later

APRIL 29, 1992
All four officers are acquitted from excessive force charges against Rodney King, sparking days of riots in Los Angeles, California

MAY 21, 1992
The Real World premieres on MTV

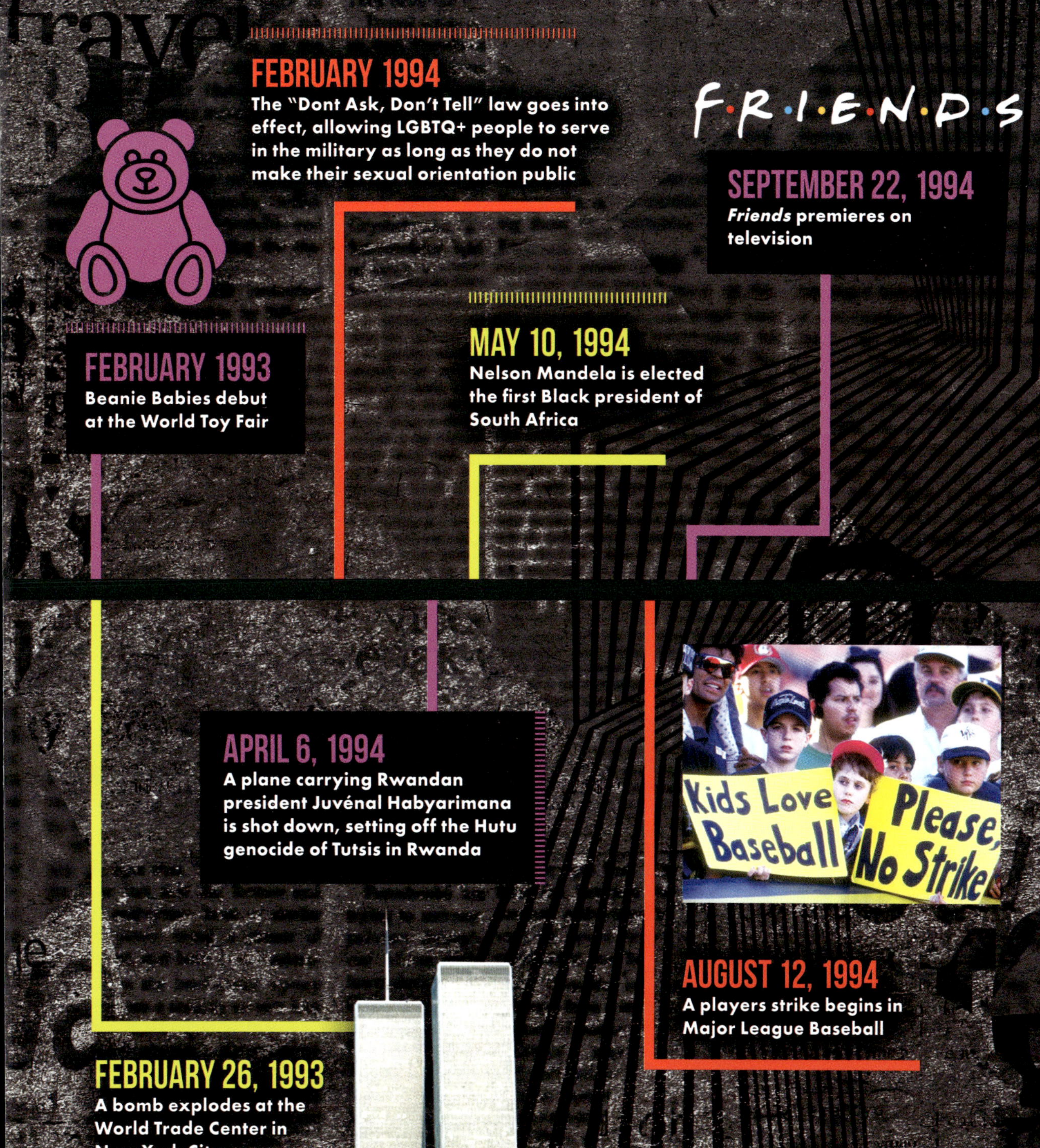

FEBRUARY 1994
The "Dont Ask, Don't Tell" law goes into effect, allowing LGBTQ+ people to serve in the military as long as they do not make their sexual orientation public

SEPTEMBER 22, 1994
Friends premieres on television

FEBRUARY 1993
Beanie Babies debut at the World Toy Fair

MAY 10, 1994
Nelson Mandela is elected the first Black president of South Africa

APRIL 6, 1994
A plane carrying Rwandan president Juvénal Habyarimana is shot down, setting off the Hutu genocide of Tutsis in Rwanda

AUGUST 12, 1994
A players strike begins in Major League Baseball

FEBRUARY 26, 1993
A bomb explodes at the World Trade Center in New York City

APRIL 19, 1995
A bomb explodes in front of the Alfred P. Murrah Federal Building in Oklahoma City, Oklahoma

SEPTEMBER 1996
Oprah Winfrey begins Oprah's Book Club

FEBRUARY 1997
Dr. Ian Wilmut announces that his team has cloned a sheep

NOVEMBER 22, 1995
Toy Story is the first full-length movie created with CGI animation

1996
A "Macarena" dance craze sweeps the U.S.

AUGUST 31, 1997
Princess Diana is killed in a car crash

JUNE 24 TO JULY 1, 1995
The first X Games are held in Rhode Island

JANUARY 23, 1997
Madeline Albright becomes the first female U.S. Secretary of State

DECEMBER 19, 1997

Titanic comes out in theaters

JUNE 14, 1998

Michael Jordan and the Chicago Bulls win their sixth NBA championship in eight years

SEPTEMBER 1, 1998

Harry Potter and the Sorcerer's Stone is published in the U.S.

DECEMBER 19, 1998

President Bill Clinton is impeached by the House of Representatives

APRIL 20, 1999

Two students kill other students and one teacher at Columbine High School in the deadliest school shooting at the time

MAY 19, 1999

Star Wars: Episode I - The Phantom Menace comes out in theaters

SEPTEMBER 11, 1999

Serena Williams wins the U.S. Open and is the second Black woman to win a Grand Slam singles title

GLOSSARY

acquitted—declared innocent of a crime or wrongdoing

activists—people who believe in taking action to make changes in laws or society

AIDS—a disease that makes a person's immune system weak and can cause illnesses to become deadly; AIDS stands for Acquired Immunodeficiency Syndrome.

apartheid—a policy that separated and discriminated against people based on their race

chromosome—part of a human cell that holds DNA

Cold War—a conflict between the U.S. and the Soviet Union in the second half of the 1900s that did not break out into fighting

communist—related to a social system in which property and goods are controlled by the government

discriminated—treated differently based on factors such as race or gender

distorted—altered from what is natural; a distorted guitar sounds more fuzzy and crushing than the natural sound.

diverse—made up of people from many different backgrounds

DNA—a tiny substance that carries information about the makeup of a living thing

endorsements—payments for promoting a product

ethnic—related to a group of people who share customs and an identity

genocides—deliberate and systematic destructions of racial, political, or cultural groups

genres—categories of a kind of art based on style, form, or content

impeached—charged a public official with a crime done while in office

jury—a group of people sworn to look into a matter of fact and give their decision

LGBTQ+—a community of people who identify as something other than heterosexual or the gender they were assigned at birth; LGBTQ+ stands for Lesbian, Gay, Bisexual, Transgender, Queer and other identities.

looting—robbing in violent situations

maximalist—style based on bright colors, bold patterns, and a more-is-more attitude

multigenerational—relating to more than one generation

nuclear war—a conflict with nuclear weapons; nuclear weapons are extremely powerful and can produce destruction quickly with long-lasting effects.

racism—the belief that race is a fundamental part of human traits and that certain races are superior to others

recession—a period of decline in economic activity, employment, and production that lasts more than a few months

republics—political and territorial units of a larger nation

riots—acts of public violence, disturbance, or disorder

selling out—compromising one's identity and beliefs for money or personal gain

skepticism—an attitude of doubt or disbelief

Soviet Union—short for the Union of Soviet Socialist Republics; the Soviet Union is a former country in Eastern Europe and western Asia made up of 15 republics or states that broke up in 1991.

terrorists—people who use fear to try to control others

transitional—marked by change

vetoed—prevented a bill from becoming law

WRITE ABOUT IT!

- What do you think were the most important moments during the 1990s? **Why?**
- Which part of the 1990s would you have liked to experience? **Why?**
- Are there any events from the 1990s that you think affect life today? **What are they?**

ALSO CHECK OUT

INDEX